Poka Yoke Error Proofing
Lean Thinking Series

SUMEET SAVANT

DEDICATION

To all Lean Six Sigma enthusiasts, practitioners, and professionals.

CONTENTS

ACKNOWLEDGMENTS

Special thanks to my wife Sahana, for always supporting me in all my endeavors and to the world of Lean Six Sigma for accepting and enabling me to perform at a global scale.

ABOUT THE AUTHOR

Sumeet Savant is a Lean Six Sigma Master Black Belt Mentor and coach, with more than a decade of experience in executing, leading and mentoring Lean Six Sigma process improvement projects. He is a BTech, MBA, and Prince certified Practitioner. He has facilitated hundreds of process improvement projects, and coached hundreds of professionals, Yellow, Green, and Black Belts over the years. He lives in Mumbai, India with his family.

LEAN

LEAN, VALUE, AND WASTE

Lean is now a common term, synonymous with process improvement, waste elimination and cost reduction.

You probably might have heard about Lean, or might have some basic idea about Lean, or might be even working on and practicing Lean methodologies

Before we start, let us understand what the term Lean really means.

Formally defined, "**Lean** is a continuous improvement strategy, focused on **maximizing customer value**, by **minimizing waste** in all the business processes, or products."

So, now the question arises, what do the terms Value and Waste mean.

"**Value**, means something, that the customer is willing to pay for, extending this definition, we can say it is something which the customer **needs, and hence expects**, from the product or service, for which he buys it.".

And, by "**Waste** we mean, any activity or feature that **does not add value** to the product or service, from the point of view of the customer."

The Japanese term for Waste so defined, is **Muda**.

Some of the examples of Waste or Muda are,

• Unnecessary travel like driving, or riding.

• Waiting for approval.

• Unnecessary Movement like bending, or stretching.

• Producing more than required.

Though Lean is primarily focused on reduction of waste, the Lean strategies framework is much broader.

To understand the Lean framework, it is a must to be well acquainted with something that is known as the **House of Lean**.

.

HOUSE OF LEAN

The collection of Lean concepts, practices, and tools, put together in a container that looks like a home, to act as a framework for implementing a complete Lean system is known as the **House of Lean.**

House of Lean: Goals

The first component of House of Lean is its roof, which represents the **Goals** of the business.

Most businesses have similar goals as follows,

• **Highest Quality**

Quality in terms of features and characteristics of the products or services provided to the customer.

• **Lowest Cost**

Lowest cost in terms of raw materials, man power, and machinery required to design, develop and deliver the products.

• **Shortest Lead Time**

Shortest time taken from initiation of idea to going to market of the products or services.

The roof of the House of quality is depicted in the following figure.

House of Lean: JIT

The next component of the House of Lean is its left pillar, which represents the **JIT or Just In Time** concepts, practices, and tools.

Just In Time

JIT is a methodology aimed primarily at reducing flow times within production system as well as response times from suppliers and to customers. It aims at reducing the inventory, and overproduction by producing just in time to meet the customer demands.

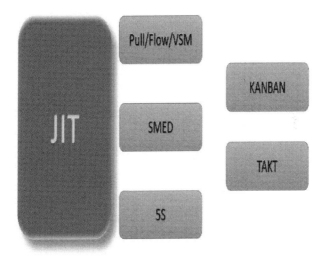

The JIT concepts, practices, and tools include the following,

• Pull

Pull means producing to the customer demand.

• Flow

In Lean, the process flow, which means to move along in a steady, continuous stream, should be free of waste, and issues, to ensure a steady continuous uninterrupted flow.

• VSM

Value Stream Mapping is a technique to chart the flow of the processes, identify wastes in the flow, establishing root causes for the wastes, and identifying ways to reduce or eliminate the wastes.

• KANBAN

Kanban is a scheduling system for lean manufacturing and just-in-time manufacturing, that makes use of cards to track, schedule and control production.

• SMED

Single-minute exchange of die, is a lean production method to provide a rapid and efficient way of converting a manufacturing process from running the current product to running the next product, it is a system for reducing the time taken for equipment changeovers.

• TAKT

TAKT Time, is the average time or rate at which a product needs to be completed in order to meet customer demand.

• 5S

5S is a workplace organization framework that uses five Japanese words to represent its principles or phases: Seiri(Sort), Seiton(Set in order), Seiso(Shine), Seiketsu(Standardize), and Shitsuke(Sustain).

House of Lean: JIDOKA

The next component of the House of Lean is its right pillar, which represents the **JIDOKA** concepts, practices, and tools.

JIDOKA

JIDOKA, also known as Autonomation which means "Intelligent Automation" or "Humanized Automation", is an automation which implements some sort of monitory techniques, making it "aware" enough to detect an abnormal situation, and stop the machine, to enable the workers to stop the production line, investigate the root causes and fix the issue.

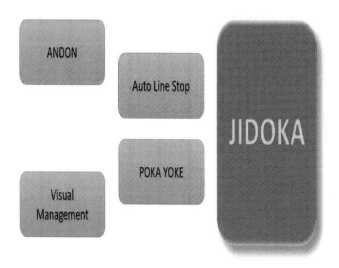

The JIDOKA concepts, practices, and tools include the following,

• ANDON

ANDON is an alerting system that notifies management, maintenance, and other workers of a quality or process problem. It can be manual or automated.

• Auto Line Stop

Auto Line Stop is a system that stops the production process whenever an issue or defect occurs, it can be automated or manual.

• POKA YOKE

POKA YOKE or Mistake Proofing, is a lean mechanism that helps an equipment operator avoid (yokeru) mistakes (poka). It eliminates product defects by preventing, correcting, or drawing attention to human errors as they occur.

• Visual Management

Visual Management is a lean system to manage production and processes through visual signs and controls.

House of Lean: Standardization and Stability

The next component of the House of Lean is its strong base, which represents the **Standardization and Stability** concepts, practices, and tools.

Standardization and Stability

Standardization and Stability, deal with standardizing the work, processes, and workplace, with an aim to consistently achieve the best, and with stabilizing the processes to avoid fluctuations and variations in output.

The Standardization and Stability concepts, practices, and

tools include the following,

• Standardized Work

Standardized Work is a work derived from best practices and lessons learned while performing the work, to do it in a most efficient way, to improve productivity and avoid rework.

• HEIJUNKA

HEIJUNKA or leveling, is a technique to level the work or production load to reduce unevenness or Mura.

• KAIZEN

KAIZEN is a continuous improvement approach based on the idea that small, continuous or consistent positive changes can reap major improvements.

House of Lean: Respect for Individual

The final and core component of the House of Lean is to establish the values of **Respect for Individual**.

Respect for Individual

Respect for Individual, deals with empowering, motivating, and supporting the workforce to effectively and consistently participate in lean methodologies to guarantee and sustain improvements.

The Respect for Individual concepts, practices, and tools include the following,

• Empowerment, Motivation, and Support

Empowerment, Motivation, and Support is a management philosophy and ideology to empower, motivate, and support the workforce to encourage them identify the areas for improvement, and participate consistently and willingly without the need to be told to do so.

• Gemba Kaizen Circles

Gemba Kaizen is a Japanese concept of continuous improvement designed for enhancing processes and reducing waste at the workplace including the workforce, or the people that work at the location. Gemba refers to the location where value is created, while Kaizen relates to improvements.

• HOSHIN Planning

HOSHIN Planning is a strategic planning process in which strategic goals are communicated throughout the company and then put into action.

House of Lean

With all the components combined, the House of Lean looks similar to the following depicted figure.

FIVE PRINCIPLES OF LEAN

There are five principles of lean, based around customer, values, quality and wastes. They are,

Define Value

To be able to understand the first principle of Lean, it is essential to know what "Value" and "Quality" are.

Value is something that the customer is willing to pay for. It is something that the customer expects from the product or service, he buys. It is something, which satisfies the customer's needs.

Quality of a product or service is the degree of value the product or service adds to the customer. It means, the degree to which the product or service satisfies the customer's needs

For a company to survive and succeed, it is essential that it understands the needs of its customers, and how its products and services can satisfy its customer's needs by providing the right quality and adding the right value.

So, it is very essential to identify and define value from the point of view of the customer, and produce products and services that deliver maximum quality, and value.

Due to this reason, the very first principle in lean states to define or identify value from the point of view of the customer.

What is valuable to customer, or what are the customer's needs can be found out by collecting the VOC or the **Voice of customer**.

There are many ways VOC can be gathered, such as interviews, surveys, and market and web analytics that can help you discover what customers seek value in.

Map Value Stream

Once you identify what the customer values in your products or services, the next step is to understand the steps and activities involved in creating the value.

The **Value stream** is the complete end to end flow of a product's life-cycle.

It starts from the getting the raw materials used to make the product, and goes on up to the customer's buying, using, and ultimately disposing of the product.

Mapping the Value Stream, in this context, is an exercise to create a flowchart or a process map of all the activities involved in the product's complete life cycle.

The **Value stream process map** thus created outlines each and every step of the process for each part of the business, right from market research, to R&D, to Design, to Development, to Production, to Marketing, to Sales and Services, etc.

Only by thoroughly studying and understanding the value stream can a company understand the wastes associated, and hence find opportunities to reduce costs and tackle issues, in manufacturing and delivery of a product or service.

Supplier and customer partnership is one of the core ideas of Lean as it helps understand the complete supply chain, and eliminate wastes and other issues from the entire value stream.

Create Flow

Once you have the Value Stream Map ready, the next step will be to create Flow.

To **Create Flow**, means to ensure that the flow of the process steps is smooth and free of interruptions or delays.

The first action to achieve this is to analyze the process map for wastes.

Once the wastes are analyzed, you can perform root cause analysis to understand the causes behind the wastes.

These causes needs to be acted upon to ensure the flow of steps and activities are smoothed and made free of any issues, problems, or bottlenecks.

Once the wastes are eliminated, you can find further ways to maximize efficiencies.

Some strategies for ensuring smooth flow include breaking down steps, re-engineering the steps, work and production leveling, creating cross-functional and multi-skilled departments, suppliers, and workforce.

Establish Pull

Once you have eliminated the wastes in the process, and created the flow, the next step would be to establish Pull.

Pull is producing as per customer demand.

Inventory and Overproduction are two of the most problematic wastes in any production systems.

The ultimate goal of the pull system is to limit stocking up the inventory, and to produce only to meet the customer demand

To achieve this, you need to effectively look at the operations of the business in reverse on the value stream maps.

The idea is to capture and analyze the exact moments as to when the customers actually need the product.

This helps to implement the JIT mode of manufacturing and operations where products are produced just in time when the customers need them.

Extending this further, this also helps to get and procure even the raw materials, just in time when the production needs them.

Pursue Perfection

Once you have eliminated the wastes in the process, created the flow, and established the Pull, the final step is to keep the improvements sustained, and ongoing.

Perfection is to achieve the absolute best in anything that the company does.

So, it is absolutely not enough to just eliminate wastes, create flow, and establish pull.

You need to develop a mindset of continual improvement.

Each and every employee should strive towards perfection, and work with an aim to deliver consistent value.

This relentless pursuit of perfection is key attitude of an organization that is "going for lean", and makes Lean thinking and continuous process improvement a part of the organizational culture.

The following figure depicts the five principles of Lean.

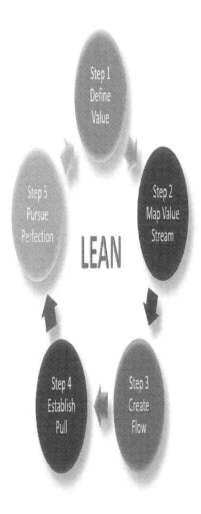

WASTES

TYPES OF WORK

Before we can understand what waste is, it is very important to understand what are the types of work.

There are three types of work based on the customer's point of view, as to how the customer looks at the work done.

They are,

• **Value Added Work**

• **Business Necessary Work**

• **Non Value Added Work**

Now, we will see each of these work types in detail.

Value Added Work

Value Added Work is the first type of work activity.

It is type of activity or work, for which the customer is willing to pay for.

Any activity which the customer perceives as actually adding value to the product or service is termed as **Value Added Work**.

These activities have the following characteristics which classify these activities as value adding.

• Change/Transformation

These activities change or transform an item from one condition to another, or from one state to another, with an overall focus of reaching the final state of the product or service, which the customer needs.

• First Time Right

These activities are done in a right way, or correctly the very first time, that is without the need for corrections or rework.

• Customer is willing to pay

These activities are activities which the customer wants done, as he perceives them to be necessary steps to create the product or service he expects, and hence is willing to pay for.

Business Necessary Work

Business Necessary Work is the second type of work activity.

It is type of activity or work, for which though the customer is unwilling to pay, still needs to be performed to create the product or services the customer needs.

This type of activity may have similar characteristics as Value Adding Activity like, transformation of an item from one state to another, or done correctly the first time.

However, the important difference which classify this type of activity differently is that the customer does not care for this activity, and hence is unwilling to pay.

Such work includes any work that might be performed to protect the business, or to comply with established policies or standards, or even as precautionary measures.

This type of work is also known as the following,

• **Business Value Added Work.**

• **Value Enabling Work.**

• **Necessary Non Value Added Work.**

Non Value Added Work

Non Value Added Work is the third type of work activity.

This work activity adds absolutely no value to the product or service.

This work activity neither transforms nor helps in achieving the end product or service.

And most importantly, the customer is not willing to pay for this work activity.

This work activity is referred to as waste, or the **Muda** in Japanese.

To figure out any non value activity in your products or service, it is best to look at them from the point of view of customer, and think whether the customer would be willing to pay for the activity.

Lean focuses on eliminating waste, by reducing or removing the non value activities from the value stream.

Example

Imagine you need to travel from one city to another, on a road.

Traveling on the road represents the value flow, as it helps you reach your destination.

Value added work would be you driving a vehicle on that road to reach your destination.

Non Value added work would be any additional turns, stops, and interruptions you may have to take while driving due to various reasons like traffic, broken pathways, pedestrians crossing roads etc.

Business Value added work would be any additional turns, stops interruptions you may have to take while driving due to the road and traffic rules like the zebra crossing, traffic lights, etc.

.

NEED TO REMOVE WASTES

Before we proceed any further, let us quickly look at a visual representation that will help you understand how important it is to remove waste from our services and products.

Consider a process, a typical process will have certain value added activities, and certain non value added activities.

Following is a depiction of a value stream of such a typical process.

Value added work is depicted in green, and non value added work in red.

This may appear quite normal, and acceptable, however just wait and watch, what happens when we analyze it.

Looking at the value stream map, we may think that it depicted a normal acceptable waste presence.

However, let us now split, and separate the value added work from the non value added work.

Now look at the newly arranged value stream map, depicted in the following figure.

You will get to clearly see what the wastes are doing to our processes.

As you can see, the minor wastes hidden here and there when taken together do appear huge, and sometimes huge enough to harm the process.

Let us continue the analysis one more step further.

Let us now actually calculate the percentage distribution of the value added and the non value added work or activity in our process.

And then let us plot the distribution in a pie chart, to get a visual feel of the percentage distribution.

Depicted below is the figure of pie distribution so created.

If you see, the total waste in our process is 43%, with so much waste hidden in our processes no wonder they are so costly.

PERCENTAGE DISTRIBUTION

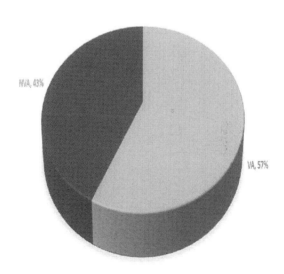

NVA, 43%

VA, 57%

■ VA ■ NVA

Lean focuses on saving these costs, by eliminating wastes and improving processes.

Imagine that the total time taken by our process is 2000 person hours, and per hour uniform cost of 50 USD.

So, the total cost of our process then would be 100000 USD

And, since 43% of the time was going waste,

The process clearly wasted as much as 860 person hour per run, and a dollar wastage of 43000 USD

If we now consider that this process runs just even once per day, just imagine the kind of loss this process is creating annually.

The reason why Lean is so powerful is that it focuses on searching such opportunities where costs can be saved.

And, as we have seen so far, to achieve the highest cost reductions in our processes, it is imperative that we need to hunt for wastes in them.

And, to hunt for wastes, we need to have a clear understanding of what the wastes are, their types, and how we can control and eliminate them.

THE 3 M'S

Any discussion on wastes, will be incomplete if we do not talk about the 3 infamous M's in the Lean world, the Muda, Muri, and Mura.

Muda

Muda in Japanese means useless, or waste, and comes in eight forms.

The figure below clearly depicts Muda, as can be seen, the truck is not being utilized to its fullest capacity, and hence considerable space is being **wasted**.

Muri

Muri is the overloading or overburdening of employees, or machines, or processes.

Employees, machines, and even processes, have thresholds or limits, which should be respected.

Trying to get more done from them, beyond their capacity, can lead to break downs or stress, and low morale.

The figure below clearly depicts Muri, as can be seen, the truck is overloaded to the point of tipping or loosing balance.

Establishing TAKT time, standardizing work, and implementing pull systems are some of the ways to avoid Muri.

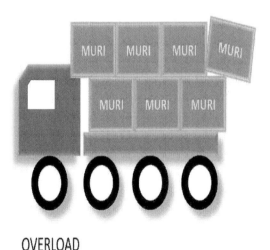

OVERLOAD

Mura

Mura is the unevenness or fluctuation or variation in the work, or workplace.

We often see this in products and services due to rushed delivery, or poor planning.

Establishing TAKT time, leveling work (Heijunka), implementing Six Sigma and pull systems are some of the ways to avoid Mura.

The figure below clearly depicts Mura, as can be seen, the two carriages of the truck are unevenly loaded.

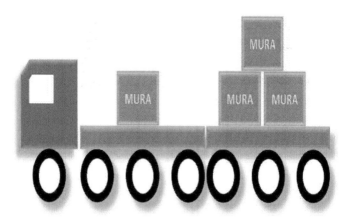

UNEVENNESS

The Ideal State

No Muda, No Muri, and No Mura is the ideal state to be achieved and sustained in any lean system.

Processes should be free or wastes, overloading, and unevenness or variation.

The figure below clearly depicts a No Muda, Muri, Mura state, as can be seen, the truck is carrying just the ideal load, free of the 3 M's.

ERRORS DEFECTS FAILURES

ERRORS

Before we can proceed with the discussion on Error Proofing, or Mistake Proofing, or Poka Yoke, it is essential we understand what are Errors, Defects, Failures and the relation between them.

To do that, let us start the discussion on Errors and cover the following topics.

• What is an Error.

• What are the different types of Error.

An **Error**, can be defined as a mistake, or an inaccuracy, or a deviation from what is correct, right or true.

Errors are the primary root cause of dissatisfaction in customers while using products and services..

TYPES OF ERRORS

Errors can be broadly classified in the following types,

• **Processing Errors** are errors that occur when process steps are either missed or incorrectly performed.

• **Setup Errors** are errors that occur when the systems, or machines, or equipment, or processes are not setup in a way that can enable their correct working. This can happen if either certain critical parts are missing, or incorrect parts are included in the setup.

• **Missing Part Errors** are errors that occur when the systems, or machines, or equipment, or processes have critical parts missing, which impacts their correct working.

• **Wrong Part Errors** are errors that occur when the systems, or machines, or equipment, or processes have critical incorrect or wrong parts present or installed, which impacts their correct working.

• **Operation Errors** are errors that occur when operations are performed incorrectly or not performed as per the established specifications.

• **Missing Operation Errors** are errors that occur when the processes, or procedures, or services are performed with critical operation(s) missing, which impacts their correct working.

• **Wrong Operation Errors** are errors that occur when the processes, or procedures, or services are performed with critical operation(s) misplaced by wrong or incorrect operation(s).

• **Missing Information Errors** are errors that occur when operations or processes are performed with critical information missing.

• **Wrong Information Errors** are errors that occur when operations or processes are performed using incorrect or wrong information.

• **Human Errors** are the skill based errors, or mistakes, or violations that humans do.

• **Measurement Errors** are errors that occur when the either the inputs or outputs of processes, or sub components of equipment, or systems, or machines, or even the results are measured incorrectly.

The following figure depicts the types of Errors for better understanding.

DEFECTS

Having understood what are Errors, now we can see what are Defects, .

To do that, we will cover the following topics in a sequence.

- What is a Defect.
- Different classifications of Defects.
- Examples and Causes of Defects..

What is a Defect

Classic definition of a **Defect** is that it is an imperfection, or a lack of something, which causes to perceive a product or service, to not be of the desired value, and not have the desired quality.

To make it simple, **Defect** can be understood as an inability of the product or service, to meet customer requirements.

Most often, it is an undesired nonconformance to either the standards, or specifications or requirements, a product or service is expected to meet, and fulfill.

And to extend this further, a Defect can also be a lack of something desired, or a presence of something undesirable, that prevents a product or a service, from performing its expected task.

Defect classification based on severity

Defects can be classified based on their severity into four classes, they are,

• **Critical** is the most severe type of defect, and renders the product or service unusable. Such defects can lead to huge financial losses, and severe injuries. This class of defects need proper analysis and fix, as they may not have a work around. Example: Failure of Brake System in a vehicle.

• **Major** is the severe type of defect, and impacts the products and services functionality and use. Such defects can cause financial loses and minor injuries. This class of defects can have work around, however they are not obvious. Example: Hard steering in a vehicle.

• **Minor** is the type of defect, that causes the products and services to provide less than desired functionality and use. Such defects hardly cause financial loses or injuries. This class of defects have some or other work around. Example: Failure of windscreen wiper system in a vehicle.

• **Low** is the type of defect, that do not impact functionality and use of products or services, however may impact the overall look, and feel. Such defects do not cause financial loses or injuries. This class of defects have simple work around, and many times do not even need work around. Example: Scratch or dent on a vehicle.

The following figure depicts the defect classification based on severity for better understanding.

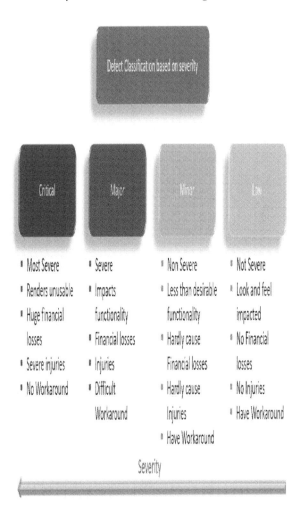

Defect classification based on priority

Defects can be classified based on their priority or urgency into 4 classes, they are,

• **Immediate** is the highest priority type of defect, and for a product or service to be usable, need to be fixed immediately. These defects need to be fixed right now, everything else can wait.

• **High** is the second highest priority type of defect, and for a product or service to be able to perform its basic function, need to be fixed urgently.

• **Medium** is the next priority type of defect, and for a product or service to be able to perform up to its level of expected function, need to be fixed as soon as possible.

• **Low** is the least priority type of defect, and the product will work even without implementing the fix, hence the fix may or may not be implemented at all.

The following figure depicts the defect classification based on priority for better understanding.

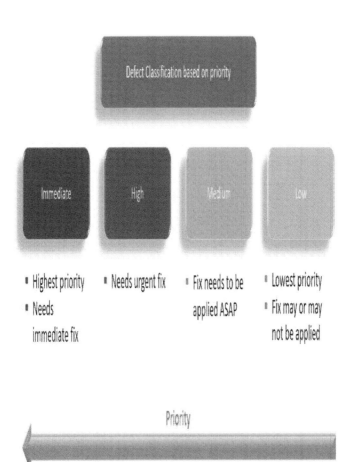

Examples and Causes of Defects

Some of the examples of Defect are,

• Lack of training or skill.

• Lack of process capability.

• Extra or over production.

• Excessive stocking up of inventory.

• Lack of concentration or focus.

• Hurried or rushed work.

• Excessive motion or transportation.

• Incomplete or inadequate testing or review.

• Improper or inadequate design strategy.

Below are some of the causes of Defects,

• Hard or Jammed Steering wheels in a vehicle.

• Spelling or typo errors in books or documents.

• Missing or incorrect information in documents.

 • Incorrect price labels on products.

 • Missed technical specifications in requirement document.

- Deleting incorrect rows or columns in tables.

- Incorrect design sent to development team.

FAILURES

Now that we have understood what an Error, and a Defect are, we can have a quick look at what a Failure means.

A **Failure**, can be classically defined as a event of something failing, in our context, it can be a product, a process, or a service.

Failure then extending the above definition can mean an event of something not working, or stopping working as expected out of it.

Failures, Defects and Errors are what causes customer dissatisfaction, and prevents products and services from delivering the desired value to the customer.

RELATION BETWEEN ERRORS, DEFECTS, AND FAILURES

Now that we know Errors, Defects, and Failure well, it is interesting to note that they are interrelated.

They share a cause and effect relationship.

Errors occur while designing, developing, or deploying products or services.

These **Errors** introduce **Defects** in them.

These **Defects** in turn causes them to **Fail** from meeting customer expectations and delivering value.

The following figure depicts the relation between Errors, Defects, and Failure for better understanding.

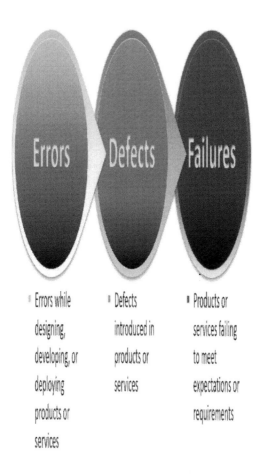

* Errors while designing, developing, or deploying products or services

* Defects introduced in products or services

* Products or services failing to meet expectations or requirements

POKA YOKE

POKA YOKE

Now that we know Errors, Defects, Failures, as well as the relation between them, it is time to understand Poka Yoke.

Poka Yoke pronounced as POH-Kah-YOH-Kay is the most effective Lean tool or methodology to prevent **Mistakes, or Errors** from occurring.

Poka Yoke was developed by Dr. Shigeo Shingo in the early 60's, as a simple technique to avoid human error at work and it went on to become the most powerful tool that could help achieve **zero defects**.

Initially it was called as **Baka Yoke** which meant Fool or Idiot Proofing, however since the term was offensive, and disrespectful, it was changed to **Poka Yoke**.

The following figure depicts the term Poka Yoke for better understanding.

Poka Yoke in broader terms

Poka Yoke in broader terms can be any of the following,

• **Zero Defect Mechanism** that helps the workers and operators to avoid human errors.

• **Prevention Mechanism** that helps to implement fail safe methods to prevent failures, defects, and errors.

• **Feedback Mechanism** that helps to implement methods to provide timely feedback to avoid failures, defects, and errors.

• **Prediction Mechanism** that helps to implement predictive methods to predict and hence prevent possible failures, defects, and errors.

• **Detection Mechanism** that helps to implement detection methods to warn and alert about failures, defects, and errors.

The following figure depicts the term Poka Yoke in broader terms for better understanding.

Poka Yoke Importance

Poka Yoke is an essential tool as it helps to,

• Prevent and avoid errors.

• Prevent, Predict, and Detect errors, defects, and failures.

• Achieve Zero Defects in processes, services, and products.

• Improve process capabilities using Six Sigma.

• Enhance process quality and performance.

• Reduced and mitigate risks when used with FMEA.

• Increase certainty, guarantee, and reliability.

Poka Yoke - When to use

And now the most important question related to Poka Yoke.

Where and When can Poka Yoke be used?

This is an important question because most often it is thought that Poka Yoke may not be used for a particular process, service, or product.

The result often times is a process, service, or product with a high probability of error.

So, to answer the question, **Poka Yoke** can be used in any,

• Process

• Service

• Product

...where an error can be made or occur.

The following figure depicts where and when Poka Yoke can be used for better understanding.

POKA YOKE PRINCIPLES

After understanding Poka Yoke, now is the good time to understand its principles.

Principles of Poka Yoke are basically the ideologies behind which the different Poka Yoke approaches work.

The principles of Poka Yoke, ordered on the basis of priority for addressing mistakes are,

- **Elimination**

- **Prevention**

- **Replacement**

- **Facilitation**

- **Detection**

- **Mitigation**

Poka Yoke Principle - Elimination

Elimination principle targets to eliminate the step or action that has the potential of error.

The idea behind this principle is that if you eliminate the error prone action(s) - then you can effectively achieve error proofing.

Elimination needs a thorough understanding of the process, to effectively pinpoint error prone steps or actions, and identifying ways for eliminating them.

Elimination often times may need redesigning, simplification and automation.

A good example for the principle of Elimination would be auto population of fields on online forms.

Another example would be doors with sensors, that work automatically instead of manual opening and closing.

Poka Yoke Principle - Prevention

Prevention principle targets to prevent the errors from happening.

The idea behind this principle is that if you put controls in your processes or products that prevent the errors from occurring - then you can effectively achieve error proofing.

Prevention needs a thorough understanding of the process, to effectively pinpoint potential error conditions, and identifying ways for modifying them in order to prevent the errors from occurring.

Hence Prevention too often times may need redesigning, simplification and automation.

A good example for the principle of Prevention would be restricting the length of characters to be entered in certain text fields on online forms.

Another example would be electronic devices that shut down due to various reasons like overheating, inactivity for certain duration, and so on.

Poka Yoke Principle - Replacement

Replacement principle targets to replace error prone steps or processes or products.

The idea behind this principle is simple and straight forward, and that is to replace your processes or products that have the probability of error with more reliable and stable processes.

Replacement needs a thorough understanding of the process, to effectively pinpoint processes, products, steps, or tasks with potential error conditions, and replacing them with better alternatives.

Hence Replacement too often times may need redesigning, simplification and automation.

A good example for the principle of Replacement would be replacing text fields with select boxes on online forms.

Another example would be dispensers of various kinds like coins, cash, packaging tapes and so on.

Poka Yoke Principle - Facilitation

Facilitation principle targets to facilitate means to make work easier and less error prone.

The idea behind this principle is that if you combine techniques and methods to facilitate performing tasks correctly and easily - then you can effectively achieve error proofing.

Facilitation needs a thorough understanding of the process, to effectively facilitate means like instructions, or color coding, or similar to avoid potential error situations, and to prevent the errors from occurring.

Facilitation too may often times need some amount of redesigning, simplification, and automation, along with ways to pass on accurate instructions.

A good example for the principle of Facilitation would be password policies enforced on online applications with specific, and clear instructions.

Another example would be color coding of parts and materials to be used on assembly lines.

Poka Yoke Principle - Detection

Detection principle targets to detect an error immediately as it occurs and providing an opportunity to correct.

The idea behind this principle is that if you add controls to proactively detect and correct the error before it is allowed to proceed - then you can effectively achieve error proofing.

Detection is different from other techniques is that you allow an error to occur, however the moment an error occurs, the control mechanism detects the errors and allows to correct the mistake, before the process can proceed further.

A good example for the principle of Detection would be any validating alerts on online forms that detect invalid formats or lengths or characters of fields and asks the users to re-enter.

Another example would be any monitoring devices that warn and alert automatically upon detection of error conditions.

Poka Yoke Principle - Mitigation

Mitigation principle targets to minimize the effect of an error as it occurs and provide an opportunity to correct.

The idea behind this principle is that that at certain times errors cannot be prevented or avoided, and in such situations along with just relying on error proofing mechanisms, it is a good idea to also be prepared to recover from an error once it occurs.

Mitigation is similar to Detection as it too allows an error to occur, however the moment an error occurs, the control mechanism provides means to revert back to the most recent or best known correct state.

A good example for the principle of Mitigation would be any backup mechanisms designed to revert back to correct state post system failure or error.

Another example would be heat activated fire sprinklers.

The following figure depicts the Poka Yoke principles for better understanding..

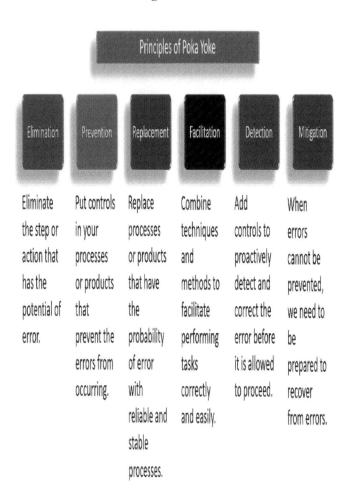

Principles of Poka Yoke

Elimination	Prevention	Replacement	Facilitation	Detection	Mitigation
Eliminate the step or action that has the potential of error.	Put controls in your processes or products that prevent the errors from occurring.	Replace processes or products that have the probability of error with reliable and stable processes.	Combine techniques and methods to facilitate performing tasks correctly and easily.	Add controls to proactively detect and correct the error before it is allowed to proceed.	When errors cannot be prevented, we need to be prepared to recover from errors.

POKA YOKE APPROACHES

POKA YOKE APPROACHES

Having understood the concept of Poka Yoke well, it is now time to look at the various Poka Yoke approaches.

Poka Yoke approaches can be classified in a number of ways, based upon the implementation strategy.

Some of the well-known **Poka Yoke** approach classifications are,

• **Poka Yoke for Prevention of errors** classified as Hard, Soft, and Andon Poka Yoke.

• **Poka Yoke based on point of Inspection** classified as Proactive, and Reactive Poka Yoke.

• **Poka Yoke for Detection** classified as Contact, Fixed-Value, and Motion-Step Poka Yoke.

• **Poka Yoke based on condition of defect** classified as Warning, and Detection Poka Yoke.

The following figure depicts the various Poka Yoke approaches for better understanding.

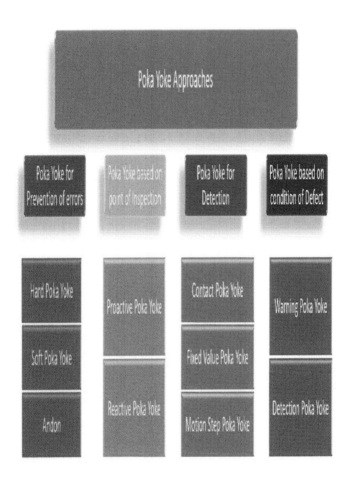

POKA YOKE FOR PREVENTION OF ERRORS

Poka Yoke that focus on preventing errors can be classified based upon the way they go about preventing errors.

Poka Yoke for Prevention of errors are most often classified as,

• **Hard Poka Yoke** approach is designed to ensure the errors are prevented.

• **Soft Poka Yoke** approach is designed to detect and warn on the error or defects as they arise, for immediate action.

• **Andon** approach is designed to detect, warn, and STOP the processes in case of errors and defects, to ensure defect pieces do not flow in the production..

Hard Poka Yoke

Hard Poka Yoke approach is built with a view to prevent errors from occurring.

It focuses on developing processes, or services, or products that ensure error free execution.

The major challenge in this approach lies in anticipating error conditions, and errors accurately, and implementing mechanisms that either prevents those error conditions, or the errors, or both from occurring.

Hence, this approach incorporates preventive actions into the process, or service, or product design.

An excellent example for the Hard Poka Yoke approach would be any online form that prevent you from proceeding further before filling all the mandatory details.

Soft Poka Yoke

Soft Poka Yoke approach is built with a view to alert the errors that are about to occur.

It focuses on developing processes, or services, or products that alert whenever any error is about to happen so that prompt action can be taken either manually or automatically to prevent an error from occurring.

The major challenge in this approach lies in anticipating error conditions, and errors accurately, and implementing mechanisms that alert whenever either the error conditions, or the errors, or both are about to occur.

Hence, this approach incorporates monitoring and alerting actions into the process, or service, or product design.

An excellent example for the Soft Poka Yoke approach would be any vehicle fuel gauge with reserve alert mechanism.

Andon

Andon approach is built with a view to alert the errors that are about to occur, and stop the execution immediately.

It focuses on developing processes, or services, or products that not just detect and alert, but also stop the processes whenever any error is about to happen so that prompt action can be taken either manually or automatically to prevent an error from proceeding further.

The major challenge in this approach lies in anticipating error conditions, and errors accurately, and implementing mechanisms that detect, alert, and stop whenever either the error conditions, or the errors, or both are about to occur.

Hence, this approach incorporates monitoring, alerting, and stopping actions into the process, or service, or product design.

An excellent example for the Andon approach would be any assembly line where the assembly line is automatically stopped upon detection of an error or error condition.

The following figure depicts the different Poka Yoke approaches for prevention of errors.

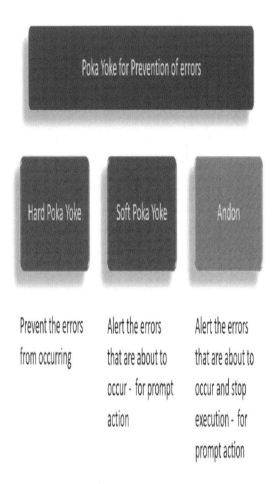

POKA YOKE BASED ON POINT OF INSPECTION

Poka Yoke that is based upon the point of Inspection can be classified based upon when the inspection happens with respect to the process execution.

Poka Yoke based on point of Inspection are most often classified as,

• **Proactive Poka Yoke** approach is designed to inspect for errors at the point of origin.

• **Reactive Poka Yoke** approach is designed to inspect for errors after the process execution.

Proactive Poka Yoke

Proactive Poka Yoke approach is built with a view to inspect for errors, and error conditions at the point of origin, and hence to prevent errors from occurring.

It focuses on developing processes, or services, or products that ensure error free execution.

The major challenge in this approach lies in identifying the points of origin of error conditions, and errors accurately, and implementing mechanisms exactly at those points, either to prevent those error conditions, or the errors, or both from occurring.

Hence, this approach incorporates preventive actions into the process, or service, or product design.

An excellent example for the Proactive Poka Yoke approach would be text fields that restrict the length, or format, or characters that the users can enter on online form.

Reactive Poka Yoke

Reactive Poka Yoke approach is built with a view to inspect for errors, and error conditions once the process execution completes.

It focuses on developing processes, or services, or products that ensures error are detected immediately after the process execution.

The major challenge in this approach lies in detecting and capturing error conditions, and errors accurately once the process is completed.

This information about the errors is then used to take corrective actions.

Hence, this approach incorporates reactive actions into the process, or service, or product design.

Though this approach does not eliminate the errors, however it does guarantee that the error does not pass on to the next process.

An excellent example for the Reactive Poka Yoke approach would be any validations that happen on online form that catch the errors on submission and allows the requester to correct the entries, before proceeding further.

The following figure depicts the different Poka Yoke approaches based on point of inspection of errors.

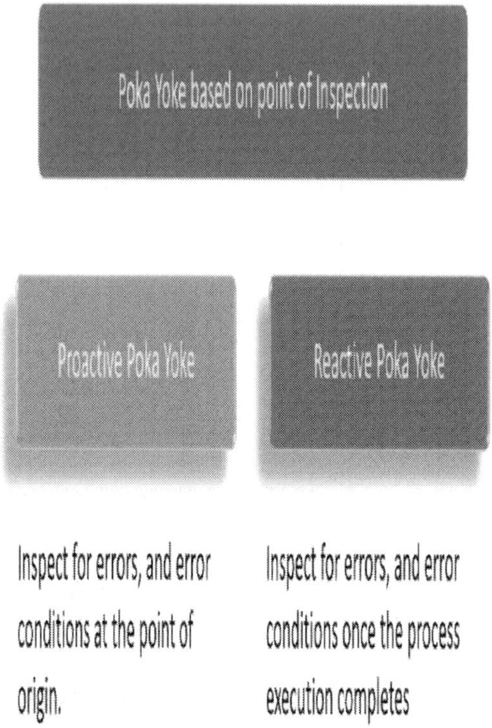

Poka Yoke based on point of Inspection

Proactive Poka Yoke

Reactive Poka Yoke

Inspect for errors, and error conditions at the point of origin.

Inspect for errors, and error conditions once the process execution completes

POKA YOKE FOR DETECTION

Poka Yoke used for detection of errors and defects can be classified based upon the method used for detecting errors.

Poka Yoke for Detection are most often classified as,

• **Contact Poka Yoke** approach is designed to detect errors using physical contact with the help of sensors.

• **Fixed Value Poka Yoke** approach is designed to detect errors using counting of repeating parts or operations.

• **Motion Step Poka Yoke** approach is designed to detect errors using process sequence to determine if any step or has occurred or is out of sequence.

Contact Poka Yoke

Contact Poka Yoke approach is built with a view to detect errors using physical contact.

It makes use of sensors that sense parts, or material, or surfaces by making physical contact, and alerts when it finds any part missing.

Situations of rapid repetition, and environmental problems can make use of this approach.

This approach is effective in identifying irregularities in product's dimensions like shape, size, or position.

Limit switches, toggle switches, photoelectric switches are excellent examples for the Contact Poka Yoke approach.

Fixed Value Poka Yoke

Fixed Value Poka Yoke approach is built with a view to detect errors using counting.

It makes use of sensors that counts the number of parts, or materials, or surfaces and alerts when it finds the count not matching the predetermined fixed value.

Situations of operators repeating the same activities or parts can make use of this approach.

This approach is effective in tracking the frequency of an operation or activity.

Limit switches that are used to count the number of holes drilled is a classic example for the Fixed Value Poka Yoke approach.

Motion Step Poka Yoke

Motion Step Poka Yoke approach is built with a view to detect errors using the knowledge of process steps sequence.

It makes use of sensors that check if a step has occurred or not as per the expected sequence and alerts when it finds any mismatch.

Situations of operators performing different activities one after another in a sequence can make use of this approach.

This approach is effective in tracking motions of each step or activity in a sequenced process.

Photo Electric switches that are used to along with timers, to alert when an activity does not happen within a predetermined time limit is a classic example for the Motion Step Poka Yoke approach.

The following figure depicts the different Poka Yoke approaches for detection of errors.

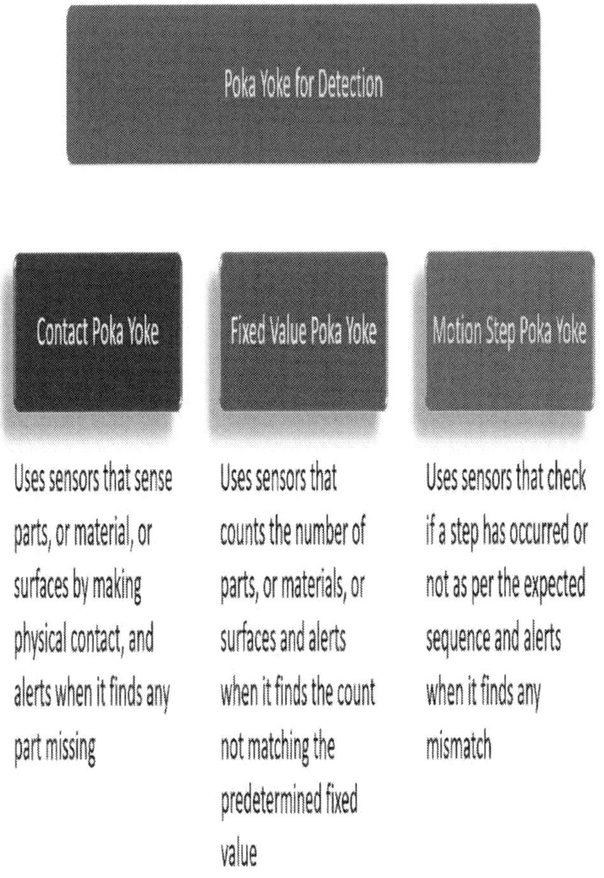

Poka Yoke for Detection

Contact Poka Yoke

Uses sensors that sense parts, or material, or surfaces by making physical contact, and alerts when it finds any part missing

Fixed Value Poka Yoke

Uses sensors that counts the number of parts, or materials, or surfaces and alerts when it finds the count not matching the predetermined fixed value

Motion Step Poka Yoke

Uses sensors that check if a step has occurred or not as per the expected sequence and alerts when it finds any mismatch

POKA YOKE BASED ON CONDITION OF DEFECT

Poka Yoke based on condition of Defect can be classified based upon the state of defect or error.

Poka Yoke based on condition of Defect are most often classified as,

• **Warning Poka Yoke** approach is designed to warn about an error that is about to occur.

• **Detection Value Poka Yoke** approach is designed to detect and act on an error that has occurred.

Warning Poka Yoke

Warning Poka Yoke approach is built with a view to warn on errors that are about to happen, whenever an error condition is approaching true.

It makes use of warning sensors to signal a problem that is going to create an error if not acted promptly.

These warning sensors can use color, alarm, light to alert on an impending error.

Whistles on pressure cookers, virus warning messages are great examples for the Warning Poka Yoke approach.

Detection Poka Yoke

Detection Poka Yoke approach is built with a view to detect and alert on errors that have happened, whenever an error condition is met.

It makes use of warning sensors to signal that an error has occurred.

These warning sensors can use color, alarm, light to alert on an impending error.

Most often this approach automatically shuts off the system as soon as an error is detected, and only once the error is corrected either manually or automatically, then the process can be continued.

This ensures the error does not proceed in the flow.

Online form validation messages are great examples for the Detection Poka Yoke approach.

The following figure depicts the different Poka Yoke approaches based on the condition of defects for better understanding.

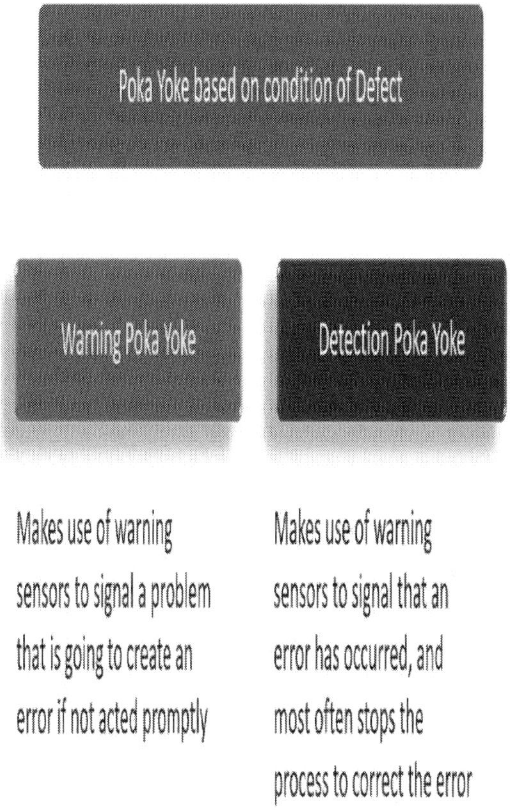

Poka Yoke based on condition of Defect

Warning Poka Yoke

Detection Poka Yoke

Makes use of warning sensors to signal a problem that is going to create an error if not acted promptly

Makes use of warning sensors to signal that an error has occurred, and most often stops the process to correct the error

POKA YOKE DEVICES

POKA YOKE DEVICES

Now that we have understood the concept of Poka Yoke, and the different Poka Yoke approaches well, we can now conclude the discussion by having a look at the different Poka Yoke devices.

Poka Yoke devices can be classified as.

• **Stop Devices** that either stop the executing process, or service, or product when abnormalities arise that may cause an error to occur, or when errors occur.

• **Control Devices** that either prevent errors from occurring, or prevent errors from flowing further the process, once they occur.

• **Warning Devices** that either warn that errors are about to happen, or signal that an error has occurred.

The following figure depicts the different types of Poka Yoke devices for better understanding.

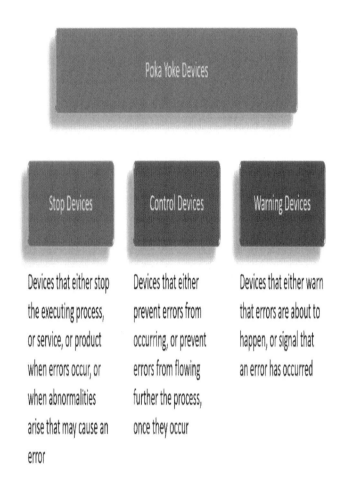

Guide Pins

Guide Pins are pins or pegs that are used for aligning a tool or die properly with the work.

Guide Pins are used for proper alignment, or proper orientation of work pieces during assembling the parts.

They are relatively easy to develop and implement.

Guide Pins are most effective for errors that occur during assembling of parts like,

• Wrong Order.

• Incorrect Selection.

• Incorrect Position.

• Incorrect Orientation.

Alerts and Alarms

Alerts and Alarms are prompts and signals of danger or emergency, that require immediate action to avoid potential errors or losses.

Alerts and Alarms are used either to warn that an error is about to occur, or to signal that an error has occurred.

They most often need sensors in processes and products, to detect error conditions.

Alerts and Alarms can be in most of forms like,

• Sirens.

• Bells.

• Horns.

• Flash Lights.

• Plain Lights.

Limit Switches

Limit Switches are automatic control switches that prevent a product or process from going beyond a predetermined limit.

Limit Switches are used for proper positioning of devices, detecting presence or absence of objects, and positioning of work pieces.

They most often require physical contact to work effectively.

Limit Switches are most effective for errors like,

• Incorrect orientation or positioning.

• Incorrect selection or counting.

• Omissions.

• Incorrect repetitions.

Proximity Sensors

Proximity Sensors are sensors able to detect the presence of nearby objects without any physical contact.

Proximity Sensors are often times used for proper positioning of work pieces, detecting presence or absence of objects, and determining levels of tanks or bins.

They most often make use of electromagnetic field or a beam of electromagnetic radiation.

Proximity Sensors are most effective for errors like,

• Incorrect orientation or positioning.

• Incorrect selection or counting.

• Omissions.

• Incorrect repetitions.

Displacement Sensors

Displacement Sensors are devices that measure the distance between the sensor and an object by detecting the amount of displacement through a variety of elements and converting it into a distance.

Displacement Sensors are often times used for measuring distances, proper positioning of work pieces, detecting presence or absence of objects, and confirming passing of objects.

They most often make use of lasers for error proofing displacement sensors.

Displacement Sensors are most effective for errors like,

• Danger Sensing failures.

• Incorrect selection or counting.

• Omissions.

Artificial Vision Systems

Artificial Vision Systems are systems that provide automated image based inspection for a variety of industrial and manufacturing applications, most often used in quality control.

Artificial Vision Systems are often times used for detecting missing parts on assembly line, poor quality components or surfaces, proper orientation and positioning of parts, and detecting colors.

They most often do not need contact, however they do need sufficient light for effective use.

Artificial Vision Systems are most effective for errors like,

• Incorrect orientation or positioning.

• Incorrect selection or counting.

• Omissions.

• Incorrect recognitions.

Counters and Timers

Counters and Timers are systems that counts something and indicates a number or amount, and times activities.

Counters and Timers are often times used for ensuring expected number of events or activities occur, and preventing failure by timing usage of the products.

They most often are much easier to use and understand.

Counters and Timers are most effective for errors like,

• Incorrect orientation or positioning.

• Incorrect selection or counting.

• Incorrect repetition.

Checklists

Checklists are comprehensive lists of things to be checked or done.

Checklists are the most effective error proofing tools that can be used for any operation, or task, or activity in which an error can occur.

They are the easiest to develop, use, and understand, hence find their use universally.

Checklists are most effective for errors like,

• Incorrect orientation or positioning.

• Incorrect selection or counting.

• Incorrect repetition.

• Omissions.

• Incorrect recognitions.

The following figure depicts the different types of Poka Yoke devices for better understanding.

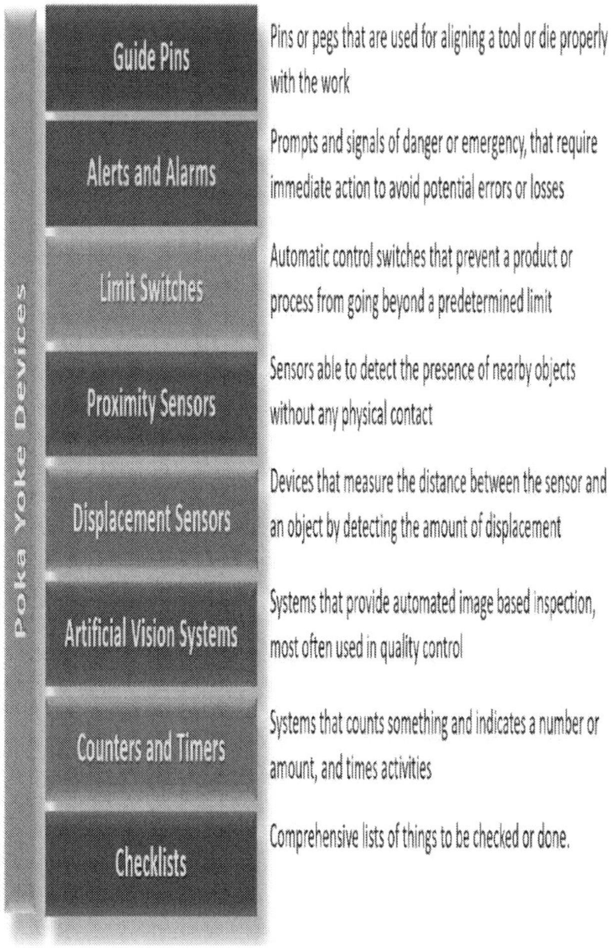

Poka Yoke Devices		
Guide Pins	Pins or pegs that are used for aligning a tool or die properly with the work
Alerts and Alarms	Prompts and signals of danger or emergency, that require immediate action to avoid potential errors or losses
Limit Switches	Automatic control switches that prevent a product or process from going beyond a predetermined limit
Proximity Sensors	Sensors able to detect the presence of nearby objects without any physical contact
Displacement Sensors	Devices that measure the distance between the sensor and an object by detecting the amount of displacement
Artificial Vision Systems	Systems that provide automated image based inspection, most often used in quality control
Counters and Timers	Systems that counts something and indicates a number or amount, and times activities
Checklists	Comprehensive lists of things to be checked or done.

AUTHOR'S NOTE

I thank you for choosing the book, I have presented to you a detailed concept of Error Proofing, different Poka Yoke approaches, and various Poka Yoke devices, following a detailed description of Defects, Failures, Errors, and the relationship between them.

I hope this adds value to you and helps you eliminate wastes, and achieve cost reductions in your processes.

Please leave a review wherever you bought the book, and it will help me in my quest to provide good useful products to you on Lean Six Sigma.

All the very best,

Sumeet Savant

Lean Six Sigma Master Black Belt and Coach

Printed in Great Britain
by Amazon

35718849R00071